CONTENTS

BRIEF  BOOKS

GOSPEL SPEECH ONLINE

Speaking the truth in love in a digital world

LIONEL WINDSOR

with an introduction by Tony Payne

 matthias media

SYDNEY · YOUNGSTOWN

INTRODUCTION: BUILDING WITH WORDS

Let no corrupting talk come out of your mouths, but only such as is good for building up, as fits the occasion, that it may give grace to those who hear. (Eph 4:29)

The idea that we should 'build' each other up with words is a common one in the New Testament (it's discussed at length in 1 Corinthians 12-14, for example). But how do words build?

At one level, it seems obvious: words can build people up, or discourage and tear them down. But building is also a strange thing to do with words, when you think about it. Words are just words, after all: they have no physical existence in the world. There are so many materials or substances you can build with in order to construct something real and substantial—bricks, cement, bamboo, LEGO. But what can you really construct or build by talking? Or, to put it another way, how do our words actually make any difference at all? Are they not just vibrations in the air? Isn't it all just... talk?

In this introduction, I want to explain how Christianity makes a vast difference to understanding how you can 'build' with words.

Playing games

Secular humanism has come to be the dominant worldview in our culture over the past 200 years. Yet often we are unaware of the ways in which that worldview trickles down into our lives and communities—particularly in how we think about words and language.

Secular humanism is the inherently dysfunctional attempt to make sense of the world and our lives without reference to the God who created everything and who gives sense, meaning and purpose to all existence. Secular humanism shuts out that idea and tries to make sense of the world without any external reference point. All we have to work with is just this physical universe that we can see, touch and experience.

But when we take away God, and the order and meaning that a creator God gives to his creation, many aspects of human life and experience become extremely difficult to explain and understand. For example, one of the problems that Western thought has had to battle is whether we can actually know anything for sure about the world. After all, the only point of contact I actually have with the world is via my senses and what my brain makes of it. But how can I possibly know if what is really out there actually matches my sense perception of it? Philosophically speaking, it's very hard to be sure. Which means I'm left with the prospect that the only thing I really know for sure is my own knowledge—and that may or may not be reliable.

This radical scepticism about our ability to really know the truth about reality leads to a further difficulty: how can we ever be sure that the words we use to describe what our senses and brain tell us is out there correspond to anything real at all?

In the 20th century, this sort of thinking led to the idea that language is really just a very complicated game with its own set of rules. We can do various things in this game (make promises, assert things, ask things, command things, and so on) and build up a complicated, but tacitly accepted, set of conventions to play this game together, but we shouldn't make the mistake of thinking that our word games actually refer to anything real outside of themselves. Words are just symbols, like playing pieces, cards or dice. We can use them for different purposes in relation to all the other people in the game, but they don't have any certain connection to something that is 'true'–something that is actually out there in the world. Words are not a means for naming something that is objectively true or real, but for making progress in the language game we're playing.

These ideas have been bubbling away in our Western intellectual cauldron for most of the 20th century. Inexorably, they have bubbled over and trickled down into the broader culture. For postmoderns, words are increasingly tools you use to exercise power in some way–to achieve something in the game that you're in. They are not a means of saying something or arguing that something is objectively true (and therefore relevant to both of us), but a means to achieve what I want to achieve– to gain an advantage in the game we're playing.

We certainly see this in how our public discourse as a community has steadily but relentlessly diminished in quality over the past fifty years. It's not former Prime Minister of Australia Tony Abbott's fault, former UK Prime Minister David Cameron's fault or US President Donald Trump's fault; it's a problem that's been brewing for a long time, and is now becoming increasingly apparent. If words have no necessary connection to truth or reality, then my task is not to persuade you of the truth through argument or evidence, but to win you to my side through spin, manipulation, PR, sloganeering, irony, humour, snarkiness, excitement, or sometimes simply by silencing the other side and not letting them speak. If you've ever had the misfortune to be part of a Facebook or Twitter argument of any length, you'll know what I mean. If you've observed carefully how our political discourse has been trending over the past two decades, you'll also know what I mean.

What I'm saying is that in the late modern or postmodern period we're in, truth is no longer the goal of speech, nor is rational or empirical argument the means to reach it. It's simply about winning the word game, and any tactic is legitimate—including the ultimate sanction, which is forbidding you to speak (usually by classifying your speech as out-of-bounds and no longer within the rules of the game). We see this happening more and more.

Building a world

Our loss of confidence in the capacity of words to represent truth is a form of madness. But that's what happens when you embrace a big fantastical lie (namely, that God is not God and did not create this world), and build a life and a worldview on it. Things fall apart; the centre cannot hold; linguistic anarchy is loosed upon the world.[1]

But the real world that is there is not the accidental, random, purposeless product of time and chance; it is the creation of a good God, who made it according to the good and wise order of his eternally good and wise mind.

Furthermore, the expression of that mind and the content of the good order by which God made the world is something that the Bible calls "the Word":

> In the beginning was the Word, and the Word was with God, and the Word was God. He was in the beginning with God. All things were made

---

1 If I may co-opt Yeats to my cause.

through him, and without him was not any thing made that was made. In him was life, and the life was the light of men. (John 1:1-4)

The world is built according to the good word of God. It bears his stamp. It really is there, and we know not only that it is there, but what it is truly like—because the God who created it has made it so and has testified that it is so.

In addition, the world has an order that expresses God's own mind and character. That's what the writer of Proverbs was talking about in this extraordinary passage:

"The Lord possessed me at the beginning of his work,
    the first of his acts of old.
Ages ago I was set up,
    at the first, before the beginning of the earth.
When there were no depths I was brought forth,
    when there were no springs abounding with water.
Before the mountains had been shaped,
    before the hills, I was brought forth,
before he had made the earth with its fields,
    or the first of the dust of the world.
When he established the heavens, I was there;
    when he drew a circle on the face of the deep,
when he made firm the skies above,

> when he established the fountains of the deep,
> when he assigned to the sea its limit,
> so that the waters might not transgress his command,
> when he marked out the foundations of the earth,
> then I was beside him, like a master workman,
> and I was daily his delight,
> rejoicing before him always,
> rejoicing in his inhabited world
> and delighting in the children of man.
>
> "And now, O sons, listen to me:
> blessed are those who keep my ways.
> Hear instruction and be wise,
> and do not neglect it.
> Blessed is the one who listens to me,
> watching daily at my gates,
> waiting beside my doors.
> For whoever finds me finds life
> and obtains favour from the Lord,
> but he who fails to find me injures himself;
> all who hate me love death." (Prov 8:22-36)

Who or what is the writer talking about in this passage? It is wisdom. 'Wisdom' is the name the Bible gives to the kind of words that explain and teach the truth about the world that God has made. If you listen to wisdom—to words that describe the way things really are—then you will find life. You will know how to live in God's world.

It's no surprise that throughout the wisdom literature of the Bible, words play such an important part in the good and successful life. True, right and apt words—the right word for the right time—bring life, healing, success and joy, because these true and wise words connect you to what is really *there*, to the good created order that God has made.

Building a life

The words of biblical wisdom, built on the fear of the Lord, are foundations for building a life upon, because they are not just signs or part of a game; they connect us with the truth about reality. What the wisdom literature foreshadowed, we see coming to a majestic fulfilment in Christ, who is God's wisdom made flesh:

> "Everyone then who hears these words of mine and does them will be like a wise man who built his house on the rock. And the rain fell, and the floods came, and the winds blew and beat on that house, but it did not fall, because it had been founded on the rock. And everyone who hears these words of mine and does not do them will be like a foolish

man who built his house on the sand. And the rain fell, and the floods came, and the winds blew and beat against that house, and it fell, and great was the fall of it." (Matt 7:24-27)

The gospel of Jesus Christ is something you can build a life on in this creation because it is the key to all knowledge: it explains where everything fits and how to understand everything. It orients you towards real life—to what is really there, to where the whole of reality is going, and to what it all means.

So to speak the truth of Jesus Christ to someone is to provide them with the material to construct a life that is solid—a life that fits with reality and participates in the kingdom of God.

As the New Testament unfolds, we see the constant importance of using words—the right words—to build other people. True words help people to understand reality, and to participate in it rightly and successfully. True words help us to construct a life that fits with how things really are.

All this radically challenges the way we speak. It challenges us to reconsider the content of what we speak in light of the truth about reality that the spectacles of Scripture allow us to see. It challenges us to reform the manner in which we speak in light of the neighbour love that Christ exemplifies and teaches. And it challenges us to rethink the goals of our speech so that they are in line with the purposes of God for us and other people.

The following chapters by Lionel Windsor explore how a Christian view of speech should be worked out in one particular sphere—the online world, in which so much speech is cast around, but so little of it builds.

Tony Payne

1. SPEAKING IN AN ONLINE WORLD

It was like living in a fishbowl, blindfolded.

It began when I entered an online conversation about a particular Christian issue. I respected all the people involved, but disagreed with some of them about the issue. To start with, the conversation seemed to be going well: it felt like we were having a genuine and friendly dialogue, with great potential to commend the gospel to people who might be reading it. But very soon after that, the dialogue descended into chaos.

Some of my conversation partners started to do bizarre things. It seemed they were saying one thing over here and the opposite over there—putting some people down while flattering others. But I could never put my finger on exactly what was happening. All I had to go on were my own impressions. After a while, I started trying to guess what their motives were. Were they trying to win the crowds? Were they playing the victim? Were they hurt, or were they on the attack (or both)?

Then I discovered that other people were making the same kind of guesses about *my* motives. I'd post what I thought was a simple comment about the matter at hand, and then I would receive replies and private messages full of unfathomable assumptions that had nothing to do with what I'd actually said. Some told me they approved of what I was trying to do; others were scathing of what I was trying to do. The problem was they all had different ideas about what I was trying to do. And none of them were right!

The actual issue we were discussing was left behind. Instead, the conversation became all about agendas and personalities. Eventually, I just didn't know how to speak any more. I wanted to say something; I had some friends who were also part of the conversation, and others who were reading the threads, who told me they were feeling confused, bullied, harassed, stupid, exhausted. I wanted to help or defend them. But how? I kept trying to engage with the issue, to listen to the participants, and to speak the truth. But before long, I found myself obsessing over every little sentence and turn of phrase. "How will this come across?" "If I say it this way, what will people think I'm trying to do?"

I realized that something had gone terribly wrong: I had started trying to speak as a Christian in this online world, and I had ended up poring over my every phrase, unable to communicate what I actually thought, feeling mute and helpless. What had gone wrong? Was it human sin in action? Was it just the medium? Maybe it was a combination of both.

When we become Christians—when we put off the old self and put on the new self—one of the key things we learn is a new way to speak. In Ephesians, Paul says:

> Therefore, having put away falsehood, let each one of you speak the truth with his neighbour... Let no corrupting talk come out of your mouths, but only such as is good for building up, as fits the occasion, that it may give grace to those who hear. (Eph 4:25, 29)

These verses are a just a small sample of a theme that keeps coming up in Ephesians: speech, or 'speaking

Christian'. Paul calls it "speaking the truth", which means speaking the gospel, speaking *in light of* the gospel and speaking *in line with* the gospel.[2] In this Brief Book, I want to focus on a particular yet increasingly important form of speech: speech in the online world.

Online communication is a huge topic, and in this book I can't even begin to cover every issue that could arise. I'm not an internet guru or a social media expert. I'm not even a true 'digital native'. I'm a minister and New Testament lecturer. I'm also a user of social media who, as my opening story shows, has made mistakes. But I've also learned some important things through it all. So in this Brief Book, I'm going to take the Bible—in particular, Paul's letter to the Ephesians—and use it to help us come to grips with what Christian speech is all about and how that affects our speech in the online world.

In this book, I'm going to concentrate on Facebook. Facebook is big and influential and affects most of us, so it's worth discussing. But I'm not going to say much about Twitter, Instagram, Snapchat, or

---

2   For more on this topic, see my earlier Brief Book, *Gospel Speech: A Fresh Look at the Relationship Between Every Christian and Evangelism*, Matthias Media, Sydney, 2015.

other platforms. That's because this book is about learning *principles* rather than specific techniques for certain platforms. Anything I say about the technology will be out of date anyway in a few months, but the biblical principles will last.[3]

So let's begin by orienting ourselves to this 'online world'–in particular, the online world of social media. The big idea of this book is that engaging with social media is just another form of speech. Yes, sometimes it can feel like it's not: there's the anonymity, the distance, the fact that the speech is happening on a screen, and so on. But when it boils down to it, it's communication. It's speech. Nevertheless, it is speech of a particular kind, with

---

3   There are a number of things I'm not going to do in this book– partly because they've been done so well by other people, for example:

- Tim Challies' *The Next Story: Life and Faith After the Digital Explosion* (Zondervan, Grand Rapids, 2011) presents an excellent overall theology of communication, and talks about how to avoid some of the personal spiritual pitfalls of online communication.
- Peter Tong has written an excellent essay on how to do theological debates; see 'Doing theology in a digital culture', in PB Bolt and T Payne (eds), *Women, Sermons and the Bible: Essays Interacting with John Dickson's 'Hearing Her Voice'*, Matthias Media, Sydney, 2014.
- For advice on protecting children see JP Steyer, *Talking Back to Facebook: The Common Sense Guide to Raising Kids in the Digital Age*, Scribner, New York, 2012.

its own strange paradoxes. So in the next chapter, we'll begin by looking at some of the paradoxes that come with this particular form of speech.

2. THE PARADOXES OF SOCIAL MEDIA

So social media is a form of speech. But it's a particular form of speech, with particular characteristics, assumptions and an ever-evolving etiquette. It's important to come to grips with some of those characteristics so we know how this form of speech works. There are great opportunities for Christians on social media to "put on the new self" and "speak the truth" (Eph 4:24, 25). But there are also huge challenges for Christians on social media to stop themselves from going back to the "old self"–the "corrupt" self with its 'corrupting' talk (Eph 4:22). A good way to get a handle on social media is to realize that it's full of paradoxes and contradictions.

1. Mediated socializing

Firstly, the phrase 'social media' is a paradox. When we say 'social', we're talking about humans being connected—people relating to one another. This is what makes social media great: it helps humans to connect—including connecting with the gospel. We are 'social beings'.[4] But there's a paradox. Normally the best kind of socializing involves true closeness and authenticity, with nothing between us. But social media is 'media', which means, literally, 'things in between': it's technology that helps people connect with other people by constantly coming between people!

2. Broadcast conversations

Secondly, social media is full of 'broadcast conversations': on social media, you have conversations, but these conversations are broadcast to other people. In practice, that means it's not quite a conversation and not quite a broadcast.

It's a conversation because people chat with each other about things. But it's not quite a conversation,

---

4   For more on this see A Cameron and S Kryger, 'Face to Face or Facebook', audio recording, Centre for Christian Living, Sydney, 20 February 2012 (viewed 12 May 2016): https://ccl.moore.edu.au/2015/01/01/listen-face-to-face-or-facebook/

because you never know who's listening in and you never quite know who's going to join in at any time. The conversation you're having is being broadcast–sent to other people, who can treat it like a broadcast show if they want. They can watch it, enjoy it, criticize it, make their own comments about it and join in if they feel like it. But at the same time, the conversation is not quite a broadcast, because it's only being sent to the people whom Facebook wants to see it.

Just think about the various reactions people have to other people's Facebook posts. I might say to Tony, "Tony, why did you share that picture of your lunch? Who cares about your lunch?!" and Tony might reply, "Because I like lunch, and I thought I was just having a conversation with a few of my friends who like lunch too. But obviously you thought it was a broadcast show and found it boring."

Or Tony might say to me, "Lionel, do you usually take this long to respond to comments about that link you shared? Don't you care about your friends?" And I might reply, "It's because I just thought I was sharing an interesting article with the world, and then I went to bed. I didn't expect the Spanish Inquisition!"

So social media is a weird hybrid of broadcasting and conversations. It's both and it's neither. I suspect that the people who are the most successful at using Facebook are the people who have come to terms with this.

3. Hyper-connected but misconnected

A third paradox of social media is that it makes us hyper-connected, but so often misconnects us. The opportunities to connect and share on Facebook are exciting, wonderful and (from a purely technical point of view) amazing. It's easy to connect with anyone anywhere in the world instantly. Wow! And there are so many wonderful opportunities for speaking the truth of the gospel. But then we realize it's also easy to misconnect. The connections happen so easily, but they're often strange, weird or awkward—or worse.

For example, you're having a conversation with a friend you know from school or church about the rain. Then someone else you know from work randomly joins in and says how outraged they are that the rain wrecked their picnic. Suddenly you're having a bizarre disagreement, and the challenge to our "old self" (Eph 4:22) is to react angrily.

4. Together alone

Fourthly, social media brings us all together, but it can also make us more alone. When you're on Facebook, you feel like you're in a universe with other people, with whom you can connect and communicate. But at the same time, we're not all actually in the same universe: we're not all on the one Facebook. Each of us has our *own* Facebook: everything is filtered and tailored to us. So you don't see what other people are seeing; you're having your own experience.

Facebook has to be filtered, of course. You can't keep up with everything your friends are saying; there's too much and you'd go mad. We need filters. Facebook filters, tailors and gives us a private experience based on what they know we like (which, of course, means they can advertise to us). But that means it's not exactly a shared experience. It's not like TV, for example. Even though Facebook feels like an online universe, it's more like a multiverse full of parallel universes, each with a population of one.

This can be a great challenge for us. Here's a hypothetical scenario: Jill has a baby and shares some baby photos. Bill is Jill's single friend. Bill says to Jill, "Your baby photos are all over Facebook. Can't you think of people who are single or struggling with infertility?" But Jill says to Bill, "Can't you share my joy? Anyway, my baby photos are not all over Facebook. What's all over Facebook is your photos of your parties, nice food and wine. I see it all the time when I'm up half the night with my screaming baby." Here are two friends who think they're in the same world, but they're not. They're together, but they're alone. And it's easy for their "old self"–the one characterized by lack of love and envy–to come out.

5. Words multiplied, communication divided

Fifthly, in social media, words are multiplied, but communication is often divided. With Facebook, you can get your point across easily, quickly and often. A few seconds of typing and suddenly your friends know what you're doing, where you are and what you care about. This is amazing and it really helps us share our message and our lives.

But speech isn't just about literal words, is it? When you hear someone, you always want to know *why* they're saying what they're saying. What are their motives? What's their purpose? In face-to-face communication, we have all kinds of social cues, we can hear the speaker's real emotions more easily and we're more likely to get their motives right. But on Facebook, when the words come to us quickly without a context and, at best, with only a cartoon emoji, we react quickly and without reflection, and we tend to automatically presume that we know the writer's purpose.

Your friend shares that they're on a plane to Melbourne. Why are they doing that? Are they boasting that they can afford a trip to Melbourne? Do they want their friends to rejoice with them that they're going to a place of culture? Or is it a cry for help: there are no good beaches any more? Maybe they just accidentally downloaded an app that automatically posts whenever they enter an airport. We don't actually know what their motives are, but we fill in the reasons. That can bring out the "old self": it can inflame conversations. You tell me you're on a plane to Melbourne. I envy you. I think you're a rich snob. And so on.

6. Manufactured authenticity

Sixthly, social media creates the paradox of manufactured authenticity. Facebook is a place to share your life. You can even share the little details. You have the opportunity to be honest, real and authentic. And that means, of course, that you can share how the truth about Jesus impacts your life.

But it's not that simple is it? Whenever you share something in this high-speed hyper-connected place, you have to think about how other people will take it. It's going to be broadcast, after all! So how's it going to come across? Are people going to read your motives correctly? Will people get the wrong idea? Will you make people sad or envious? You have to consider those things. But that means your authenticity needs to be calculated.

That has a dark side: the actor George Burns once said, "In acting, sincerity is the key. If you can fake that, you've got it made." In social media, sincerity is the key. And if you've worked out exactly how to appear authentic to other people—if you know how to get liked—if you can fake the cues so people really see how authentic you are—it's no longer the truth.

7. Controlled freedom

Finally, social media is controlled freedom. Facebook gives you great freedom: you can see so many ideas and connect with so many people easily, at a click. It's like flying. But we need to remember that Facebook is a highly controlled world. It's like the

Matrix movies: the premise of *The Matrix* is that sentient machines have placed humans in a gigantic virtual reality game where the humans live a virtual life, while the machines feed off their energy, using them as batteries.

Facebook is bizarrely similar. This isn't a conspiracy theory (I know Mark Zuckerberg isn't actually a sentient machine). But we need to realize that Facebook is a business: it uses us. Facebook makes money by feeding off our conversations. Conversations create 'energy' for them—that is, clicks—which means advertising revenue. It's not free; we are the product.[5]

The challenge for us putting off our 'old selves' is that angry, heated conversations generate even more energy for Facebook. They want you to talk outrageous drivel because that's more interesting and will get more conversations going, which will cause more people to click. They want things to be public, not private, and they'll fight with you to make that happen, literally changing your privacy settings.

---

5 "If you're not paying for something, you're not the customer; you're the product being sold"—Andrew Lewis writing on Meta-Filter, cited by E Pariser in *The Filter Bubble: What the Internet Is Hiding from You*, Penguin, London, 2011, p. 21.

And they will show you things—things not in line with the truth in Jesus—things they want you to click on.

So the online world of social media is complex. Not surprisingly, people have reacted differently to it. On the one hand, there are the embracers—those who see the opportunities of social media: "It's a new world, full of promise! It's where people are at. We should embrace and use this media for all we're worth!" Embracers take into account the opportunities. But they can be naïve when it comes to the challenges.

On the other hand, there are the naysayers: they see the world of social media as evil, twisting our message and our lives so much that it is pointless to be a part of it.[6] The naysayers have a point: they see the challenges. But they don't see the opportunities. Facebook has billions of users. It's where people are at. Can we and should we leave this world behind?

Less extreme than the naysayers are the conscientious objectors—people who deliberately

---

6 See 'Harbingers of gloom and glory: Christian responses to media technology', in A Byers, *Theomedia: The Media of God and the Digital Age*, Cascade, Eugene, Oregon, 2013, pp. 29-41.

leave social media behind because it's bad for them. There's Essena O'Neill, an Australian teenager who had half a million followers on Instagram, but who realized that the drive for attention was consuming her, so she quit.[7] There's Louis CK, who quit Twitter because it made him depressed.[8] There's Tina Fey and Amy Poehler, who deliberately don't use social media.[9] Similar points are often made by Christians too.[10]

Running away from social media may well be something you need to do too. If that's you, do it.

---

7   E Hunt, 'Essena O'Neill quits Instagram claiming social media "is not real life"', *The Guardian*, 3 November 2015 (viewed 12 May 2016): www.theguardian.com/media/2015/nov/03/instagram-star-essena-oneill-quits-2d-life-to-reveal-true-story-behind-images

8   J Blistein, 'Louis C.K. on why he quit Twitter', *Rolling Stone*, 16 April 2015 (viewed 12 May 2016): www.rollingstone.com/tv/news/louis-c-k-on-why-he-quit-twitter-20150416

9   K Dries, 'Non-social media users Tina Fey and Amy Poehler cover *Glamour*'s "social" issue', *Jezebel*, 1 December 2015 (viewed 12 May 2016): www.jezebel.com/non-social-media-users-tina-fey-and-amy-poehler-cover-g-1745445433

10 A Jacobs, 'My year in tech', *Snakes and Ladders*, 23 December 2015 (viewed 12 May 2016): www.blog.ayjay.org/uncategorized/my-year-in-tech/; and 'I'm thinking it over', *The American Conservative*, 4 January 2016 (viewed 12 May 2016): www.theamericanconservative.com/jacobs/im-thinking-it-over/; cf. J Taylor, 'The 8-point social-media apostasy of Alan Jacobs', *The Gospel Coalition*, 4 January 2016 (viewed 12 May 2016): www.thegospelcoalition.org/blogs/justintaylor/2016/01/04/the-8-point-social-media-apostasy-of-alan-jacobs/

You're allowed to. There's no law that says you *have* to be on Facebook (at least, not yet)!

But there's another reaction, which I think has a lot of merit. This is the 'disciplined user': people who don't see social media as inherently evil, but realize we need to regulate it and discipline ourselves to not have too much of it.[11] They advocate practices that include removing apps from our phones, not being connected all the time, keeping the smartphone away from the bedroom, and taking whole days off social media to enjoy the sunshine. If you take this approach, I think you could go a long way towards avoiding the pitfalls and making use of the opportunities of social media.

These are some of the paradoxes and approaches to social media. In the next chapter, we'll look at how to speak Christian in the online realm.

---

11 J Dyer, 'New year's technology resolutions of the internet famous', *Don't Eat The Fruit*, 5 January 2016 (viewed 12 May 2016): www.donteatthefruit.com/2016/01/new-years-technology-resolutions-of-the-internet-famous/

3. SPEAKING CHRISTIAN

In the previous chapter, we looked at some of the paradoxes of and approaches to social media. All of that raises an important question: how exactly do we Christians make the most of opportunities on social media? What does it mean to speak Christian in this online world?

1. The word of truth

Ephesians has a lot to tell us about what it means to speak Christian. Firstly, it tells us that there is definitely something worthwhile to speak. In Ephesians, Paul calls this message "the word of truth". It's a word that has come to Christians and turned our world upside down: "In him you also, when you heard the word of truth, the gospel of your salvation, and believed in him, were sealed with the promised Holy Spirit..." (Eph 1:13).

The "word of truth" is another way of talking about the gospel. What is the gospel? First and foremost, it's a message about salvation: it tells us that there is rescue and relief from something. What are we rescued from? Ephesians 2:1-10 says we're rescued from the futile life of this world, from our sins and the greed and envy of this world, from God's wrath against our sin, and from being under the control of the powers of this world. We've been forgiven through Jesus' death for us. And we've been made alive. That is, we've been given a new life, which is secure, because our true status is that we are actually seated with Christ, far above all rulers and powers (Eph 1:21), and we've been given a whole new life to live—a life in which to honour God and to walk and talk in new ways. This is the "word of truth" in Ephesians—the gospel message (Eph 1:13). And when Paul refers to 'truth' in Ephesians, he's talking about this gospel message and the implications of that gospel message in our lives.[12]

---

12 PT O'Brien, *The Letter to the Ephesians*, Pillar New Testament Commentary, Eerdmans, Grand Rapids, 1999, pp. 473-4.

How does this "word of truth"–this gospel truth–come? God has broadcast it to the world. But he didn't broadcast it like a TV show; God doesn't just beam the gospel into everyone's heads. No, this gospel truth, in God's wisdom, is broadcast through human beings. In a sense, God uses human beings as 'social media'.

Firstly, there's Paul himself: he's an apostle of God and he calls himself a "minister", which actually means something like a 'go-between':

> Of this gospel I was made a minister [or 'go-between'][13] according to the gift of God's grace, which was given me by the working of his power. To me, though I am the very least of all the saints, this grace was given, to preach to the Gentiles the unsearchable riches of Christ... (Eph 3:7-8)

But it's not just Paul who brings this word of truth. In Ephesians 4, we see that Christ equips the saints for the "work of ministry"–that is, Christ creates a whole people who are to be a kind of social medium: "And he gave the apostles, the prophets, the evangelists, the

---

13 JN Collins, *Diakonia: Re-Interpreting the Ancient Sources*, Oxford University Press, Oxford, 1990, p. 233; cf. pp. 77-132, 233.

shepherds and teachers, to equip the saints for the work of ministry, for building up the body of Christ" (vv. 11-12). Indeed, all Christians need to be ready to act as God's 'social media', knowing and speaking the truth: "Stand therefore, having fastened on the belt of truth, and having put on the breastplate of righteousness, and, as shoes for your feet, having put on the readiness given by the gospel of peace" (Eph 6:14-15). We're all commanded to be part of God's great spiritual battle by wearing the "belt of truth"– that is, the gospel. Furthermore, the command for us to put on those gospel shoes is about preaching the gospel, like in Isaiah 52:7: "How beautiful upon the mountains are the feet of him who brings good news, who publishes peace".[14]

At the end of his letter to the Ephesians, Paul returns to his special role as a mediator of the gospel. He asks the Ephesians to "[pray] also for me, that words may be given to me in opening my mouth boldly to proclaim the mystery of the gospel, for which I am an ambassador in chains, that I may declare it boldly, as I ought to speak" (Eph 6:19-20). Notice how Paul feels the urgency to speak this

---

14 O'Brien, p. 477.

message. The world is in darkness and in need of the gospel message. People need to hear that message in order to be saved from sin and God's wrath, and in order to have life. This salvation comes by a message–a word. It's a word that needs to get out there. It needs to be broadcast. And God uses people to do just that.

By the way, notice how Paul also uses technology: Paul's letter to the Ephesians is a letter–an ancient social medium. Paul uses this ancient social medium to encourage his church and get this message to others. The same is true today: people need this message. That's why Christians need to be online– or, at least, some of us do. There are real people in the online world, and these people need to hear (or read!) the saving gospel of Jesus Christ. If we Christians aren't there with them, they will not hear this truth of the gospel. All they will hear is the 'noise'–the endless frivolous chatter, the corruption of the old self.

Social media creates opportunities for the saving gospel of Jesus Christ to be broadcast and heard by people who otherwise might not know of him. Even better, it's a medium that isn't just for the 'experts'; it's for everyone to use. You don't have to be a professional speaker to say something about the gospel of Jesus Christ on social media; you just need to know Jesus and speak.

But there are challenges too: because anyone can use this medium, there are many opportunities for misinformation, slander, corruption, lies, degradation and worse to be given a voice, perpetuated and believed. That noise can drown out the truth far too easily. The gospel is a message of peace: peace between people and God, and peace between one another. But Facebook feeds on controversy and drivel. Facebook fans the flames of anger, but tends to quench the words of peace. So it can be hard for the gospel to get a hearing. The challenge for us Christians is to try to speak the gospel online and make clear that the gospel opposes many of the world's values, without getting caught up in the anger and needless arguments.

2. Speaking the truth in love

This leads us into my next point, which is summed up by an important phrase found in Ephesians 4:15. At this point, Paul is talking about what the truth of the gospel does to us when we hear it and believe it: the gospel doesn't leave us as isolated individuals;

the gospel actually unites us to Jesus Christ and gathers us together into a church, which Paul describes as a body. That body is the place where the truth makes its biggest impact and grows:

> Rather, speaking the truth in love, we are to grow up in every way into him who is the head, into Christ, from whom the whole body, joined and held together by every joint with which it is equipped, when each part is working properly, makes the body grow so that it builds itself up in love. (Eph 4:15-16)

The phrase I'd like to focus on is "speaking the truth in love". The original is actually "truthing in love", but clearly the truth is a spoken message. Sometimes people use the phrase 'speak the truth in love' to mean something like 'say true things in a nice way'. That's not wrong, but "speaking the truth in love" is far more than that. That truth isn't just any old truth; it's the gospel. And "in love" isn't only about the way we speak; it's about the whole context and arena of our truth-speaking. It's a network of loving relationships in the body of Christ, created by the love of God himself (Eph 1:4-5).

This love of Christ is enormous and something that Christians need to grasp. Paul prays:

> ...that you, being rooted and grounded in love, may have strength to comprehend with all the saints what is the breadth and length and height and depth, and to know the love of Christ that surpasses knowledge, that you may be filled with all the fullness of God. (Eph 3:17b-19)

So in Ephesians, the meaning of "speaking the truth in love" is more like: speaking the gospel, speaking the implications of the gospel and speaking in a gospel-shaped way within the whole network of loving relationships characterized by God's love for us in Jesus, which should be seen most clearly in the church, where that love is lived out in the presence of one another.[15] Speaking Christian happens in the context of loving relationships.

Speaking Christian online, then, means speaking the truth in the context of loving relationships. What opportunities are there for us to do this in the world of social media? I'll explore some of these in my next chapter.

---

15 ibid., pp. 310-12.

4. OPPORTUNITIES IN THE ONLINE WORLD

What opportunities does the online world create for us to speak the truth in the context of love? Well, social media creates connections for you. It's not just broadcasting, it's relationships: you have a network of relationships–'friends'–and when you post, you speak into this context. Yes, it's not the same as being physically present, and it has problems, which we've talked about a bit already. But it also gives people a connectedness that they might not otherwise have had–especially people who would otherwise be isolated by their location or life circumstances. I'm in touch with all sorts of people I would have forgotten otherwise, and in a small way, I have the opportunity to speak the truth in the context of these online relationships.

1. Speak the truth

Paul says, "Therefore, having put away falsehood, let each one of you speak the truth with his neighbour, for we are members one of another" (Eph 4:25). What is "speaking the truth" here? In one sense, it's just generally being honest. But it's more than that: we have to put away the 'lie' that the devil holds the world captive to—the lie of the world that life is found in greed and living for yourself. We don't have to pretend any more; we have the truth—the truth that we were sinners under God's wrath, that we have been saved by grace, and that we have a life that's secure and found in God and a relationship with his Son Jesus Christ (Eph 2:3-5, 4:23-24).

On Facebook, if you aren't anchored to the truth of the gospel, you have to keep lying about yourself. You have to project an image to make people like you and commend you and to make you feel good about yourself. But if you remember and believe the truth of the gospel, you can and should be honest—honest about the fact that you're a failure and a sinner, and that life's hard. But God's shown you grace: you're actually secure with Christ and that's fantastic. You don't have to do any photoshopping or airbrushing—of your profile pictures or your life. You can speak the truth.

I know Ephesians 4:25 needs to be applied firstly to how we speak to fellow Christians. But that's the beauty—and the challenge—of social media: you can't easily separate what you say to Christians from what you say to non-Christians. Facebook doesn't respect those kinds of boundaries. If you speak the truth, you're essentially speaking the truth both to Christians and non-Christians. If you hide the truth, you hide it from both. But if you are just honest in light of the gospel, that's powerful.

2. Walk in the light

Paul also talks about Christian behaviour—our actions and speech—as "light":

> ...for at one time you were darkness, but now you are light in the Lord. Walk as children of light (for the fruit of light is found in all that is good and right and true), and try to discern what is pleasing to the Lord. Take no part in the unfruitful works of darkness, but instead expose them. For it is

> shameful even to speak of the things that they do in secret. (Eph 5:8-12)

Like the world, the online world is full of darkness—darkened hearts that don't know the love of God and haven't experienced (or won't experience) God's love and the honesty and truth that it brings. But the truth of the gospel shines a big light on that darkness. Notice that it's not just the gospel that's called "light" here: we Christians are also called "light" (v. 8)!

Light illuminates the darkness. On Facebook, simply speaking the truth—speaking about your life in light of the gospel—is like a light shining in the darkness. Posts of joy in the midst of sorrow—posts of thankfulness to God in the midst of darkness—are like opening up the curtains in a dark room and letting the bright morning light flood in.

Light also exposes the darkness and shows it up. There's certainly a place for speaking about an issue or getting involved in an exchange or a disagreement. But when you do, make sure that the truth of the gospel and your life in light of the gospel shines brightly. Ultimately it will be that light and not your clever arguments that will expose the darkness.

On social media, we have the opportunity to speak the truth and walk in the light as people of the light. Sounds simple, right? Unfortunately there is always the challenge of the "old self" coming back again—something I'll explore in the next chapter.

5. CHALLENGES IN THE ONLINE WORLD

In the online world, we should aim to speak the truth and walk in the light as the children of light. But online speech has its challenges. Many of these challenges can be found explicitly in Ephesians. Ephesians talks a lot about the pitfalls for Christians—the traps and sins of our "old self" (Eph 4:22) that stop us from speaking in a godly way.

1. Sinning in anger

Firstly, there's the challenge of not sinning in anger. In Ephesians 4:26-27, Paul says, "Be angry and do not sin; do not let the sun go down on your anger, and give no opportunity to the devil". We've already seen that part of the problem of online speech is that it is, in many ways, disembodied. Speaking the truth online in the context of loving relationships is harder, because the means of relating itself can be shallower. The socializing is mediated, the conversations are broadcast, there are misconnections everywhere and the non-verbal communication cues are gone. That makes getting angry so much easier–not just righteously angry, but sinfully angry–angry with those people out there who are just *wrong*. Ephesians tells us not to let the sun go down on our anger. In other words, don't let the anger fester. Sometimes that means stopping our involvement in an online conversation and maybe picking up the phone or arranging a personal chat. At the very least, it involves praying and remembering that we are all sinners in need of grace.

2. Sinning in selfishness

Secondly, there's the challenge to be mindful of others. In Ephesians 4:29, Paul writes, "Let no corrupting talk come out of your mouths, but only such as is good for building up, as fits the occasion, that it may give grace to those who hear". Notice his emphasis on thinking about others when you speak. This is other-person-centred speech: you are not thinking of yourself, but of what is good for others. This is a huge challenge in the online world, because the 'others' aren't physically present, so it can seem like you're by yourself. Your selfishness can take over. You just want to look good. You just want to be liked.

But as Christians, our motivation in speaking is not to make ourselves look good; it's to help and build others through our speech. That means we might not be liked. Not being liked: that's the worst possible fate on Facebook! But the gospel reminds us that we don't *need* to be liked on Facebook! People who crave being liked are insecure. We're all emotionally insecure in some way, but the gospel reminds us that in actual fact, we're as secure as we can possibly be, because *God* has loved us and rescued us. We're not just 'liked' by God; we're *loved* by God. We're seated with Christ above all rulers, above all authorities and above Facebook—above the people we fear and the people whose attention we crave. So when you post and comment, pray and consider why you are doing it. Is it to build others up and give grace to those who hear? Your security in Christ means you can do that.

3. Grieving the Holy Spirit

This is a very serious matter: if you are not speaking to build others up, you are actually grieving the Spirit. Consider the next verse: "And do not grieve the Holy Spirit of God, by whom you were sealed for the day of redemption" (Eph 4:30). If we are not speaking to build others up, we are not speaking in line with the word of truth–the gospel, through which the Spirit came to us in the first place. Isn't that a terrible thing!

A clear way to ensure that we're speaking to build others up appears in the next few verses: "Let all bitterness and wrath and anger and clamour and slander be put away from you, along with all malice. Be kind to one another, tenderhearted, forgiving one another, as God in Christ forgave you" (Eph 4:31-32). Please consider printing these verses out and putting them on the back of your phone or on your computer screen. Then before you post or comment, just run what you're about to say by these verses. Are you being kind? Or are you bitter? Are you angry? Are you seeking to slander someone?

We need to be different in this regard. Instead of grieving the Spirit by our speech, we should be filled with the Spirit in our speech:

And do not get drunk with wine, for that is debauchery, but be filled with the Spirit, addressing one another in psalms and hymns and spiritual songs, singing and making melody to the Lord with your heart, giving thanks always and for everything to God the Father in the name of our Lord Jesus Christ... (Eph 5:18-20)

Our singing, prayer, thanksgiving–these are forms of speech too, and what Paul says about them also applies online. Christians talk differently; we should be seen and heard as people who talk differently.

Having thought about some of the traps and pitfalls to our 'old selves', in the next and final chapter I turn my attention to some of the practical things we can do when speaking Christian online.

6. LEARNING TO SPEAK

So how can we speak the truth in love in this online world? Here are some practical tips that arise from the things we've looked at in the previous chapters.

1. Don't let the medium master you

In chapter 2, we saw how social media is full of paradoxes. Facebook is a great way to stay in touch with friends and ideas, but it's also a dangerous medium that fractures human relationships for the sake of advertising revenue and profit. They want you online, they want you hooked, and they want to keep you insecure (or angry) so that you will keep coming back for more to get your fix. Don't let them do that to you. Of course, use the medium for the sake of speaking the truth in love. But don't let the medium use *you*.

Sometimes you need to break out of the medium entirely. Take the red pill and leave the matrix. Go offline. You're still officially allowed to. There's no law yet that says that if somebody says something on Facebook, you have to respond on Facebook! There are still other media in the world. Give the person a call. Offer to meet. Send an email. Speaking the truth in love can mean affirming the relationship by a voice on the phone or a bodily presence.

Sometimes you just need to slow it down a bit. Of course, Facebook doesn't want you to slow down, because it means they lose advertising revenue. So they will make it difficult for you, and you need to be deliberate about countering their influence. For example, don't keep your phone in the bedroom. Perhaps consider removing Facebook from your phone entirely and just use it on a more cumbersome device, like a laptop. Think about disabling all your notifications and checking the app once a day during a certain, defined period. Will that mean missing something on Facebook? Probably. Does that really matter? No.

Here's another idea: before you post or comment on anything, make a habit of showing a trusted friend or your spouse (if you have one) what you're going to post or write. They can often see things you might not see, and ask you questions about why you're writing what you're writing.

2. Don't assume you can read people's motives

In chapter 2, we also explored how difficult it is to read other people's motives online. The regular social cues that we rely on in face-to-face conversation just aren't there. You might be very good at 'reading' people in face-to-face conversations, but that ability might lull you into a false sense of your own powers, causing you to think you'll also be good at 'reading' people online. But it doesn't work that way. In fact, it is foolish and dangerous.

You should never think, "Ah, they said X, but I know they really meant Y" about someone who's writing online, unless you have a good (i.e. objective) reason to do so. Certainly you should never announce to the world that other people have false motives, unless they themselves have explicitly confessed it. That would be slander, one of the sins that grieves the Holy Spirit (Eph 4:30-31). An important way to love others in your speech is to respond to the words that people have actually said, not to the motives you are making up in your head. When you attribute motives to someone without any evidence, it usually reveals more about your own heart than it does about theirs.

3. Speak the gospel

Does this mean we should avoid online speech entirely? Not at all! In chapters 3 and 4, we saw how important it is to speak the gospel, the "word of truth" (Eph 1:13), to others. How can you do that online (particularly on Facebook)?

Firstly, you can simply just speak the plain old gospel, or share or like the posts of other people who are speaking the gospel. That is, you can say that Jesus is Lord, and that he died for our sins and rose from the dead. You can put up Bible verses. You're allowed to do that. There are no laws stopping you.

Secondly, you can speak about your life in light of the gospel. You can be intentionally thankful to God for good things. You can share the highs and lows of following Jesus. You can talk about how you're glad someone forgave you for that bad thing you did. You can express your security in Jesus. You can grieve sin. You can throw up interesting questions that relate to aspects of the gospel, like where the world's heading. And in the midst of it all, you can just have fun, because social media works best when you're having fun.

This second way of speaking the gospel is less direct than just saying, "Jesus died for our sins", but on Facebook it can get much further. That's because it's a 'human interest' story that people want to read: your friends get to know both you and, more importantly, what the gospel does for you.

Thirdly, you can speak about (or share or like) particular issues that the gospel has an impact on. A word of caution, though: when you do engage in these issues, you need to be very careful about how you speak. I'd suggest entering into these debates sparingly, carefully, prayerfully and in an informed way, and that you keep watching, first and foremost, that the gospel itself is not drowned out in your zeal for a particular issue.

Of course, you need to speak the gospel to yourself too. We should approach the online world in the same way we approach all our relationships and conversations: prayerfully conscious of the gospel of Jesus Christ. The gospel tells us that we are as secure as we can possibly be—saved by grace (Eph 2:8-10).

Because we have been loved, we can speak the truth in love. That means you should keep remembering to speak (or not speak) out of a desire to love others, not out of a desire to be *liked* by others.

4. Examine yourself

In chapter 5, we saw how social media can amplify the opportunities for the "old self" (Eph 4:22) to make an appearance. If you're using it a lot, you need to be asking yourself regularly whether you are in danger of the particular pitfalls that can come from using social media.

Maybe you need to set up a weekly reminder to do a 'spot check' on yourself. Ask yourself, "Am I reacting too quickly and angrily to people who upset me?" Am I starting to feel envious of the lives of others? Am I starting to 'manufacture' my image, faking it so that I appear 'authentic' to others? Am I speaking out of a desire to be liked, or out of a desire to love? Is there, in my heart or in my comments, any bitterness? Anger? Slander?" Keep bringing your speech to God, and asking him to change you and make you more like him.

5. Remember the true fight

I want to finish with an important reminder: Ephesians 6:10-20 tells us that we're engaged in a spiritual battle. The gospel, the truth and the word of God are key weapons in this battle. A friend of mine who was bullied online once described Facebook as the pit of hell. In some ways, it is. That's not because Facebook is particularly possessed by Satan; it's because Facebook is just a part of the world, and the world is temporarily under Satan's control (Eph 2:1-3). But we have these weapons: the word of truth, the gospel of peace, righteous lives changed by the gospel. We have the shield of faith, the helmet of salvation, and the sword of the Spirit, the word of God, and we must pray at all times in the Spirit (Eph 6:10-20). Facebook is a great place to wield these weapons as we "speak the truth in love" for the glory of God (Eph 4:15).

Feedback on this resource

We really appreciate getting feedback about our resources—not just suggestions for how to improve them, but also positive feedback and ways they can be used. We especially love to hear that the resources may have helped someone in their Christian growth.

You can send feedback to us via the 'Feedback' menu in our online store, or write to us at info@matthiasmedia.com.au.

Matthias Media is an evangelical publishing ministry that seeks to persuade all Christians of the truth of God's purposes in Jesus Christ as revealed in the Bible, and equip them with high-quality resources, so that by the work of the Holy Spirit they will:

- abandon their lives to the honour and service of Christ in daily holiness and decision-making
- pray constantly in Christ's name for the fruitfulness and growth of his gospel
- speak the Bible's life-changing word whenever and however they can—in the home, in the world and in the fellowship of his people.

Our resources range from Bible studies and books through to training courses, audio sermons and children's Sunday School material. To find out more, and to access samples and free downloads, visit our website:

www.matthiasmedia.com

How to buy our resources

1. Direct from us over the internet:
 – in the US: www.matthiasmedia.com
 – in Australia: www.matthiasmedia.com.au

2. Direct from us by phone: please visit our website for current phone contact information.

Register at our website for our **free** regular email update to receive information about the latest new resources, **exclusive special offers,** and free articles to help you grow in your Christian life and ministry.

3. Through a range of outlets in various parts of the world. Visit **www.matthiasmedia.com/contact** for details about recommended retailers in your part of the world.

4. Trade enquiries can be addressed to:
 – in the US and Canada: sales@matthiasmedia.com
 – in Australia and the rest of the world:
  sales@matthiasmedia.com.au